U S Coins Wanted

Regular Issue

Thomas Saunders

Thomas Saunders

ISBN:978 09 1430312-1

Glendower Media
P O Box 661
Whitmore Lake, Michigan 48189
www.glendowermedia.com

DEDICATION

This book is for all of you average collectors out there who go to shows, swap meets, yard sales and estate sales looking to fill the blank spots in their collections. You need to know just what you need to complete a run of dimes or nickels, and you need to have that info at your fingertips. This if for all of you who hunt for that last great coin in an unlikely place.

CONTENTS

	Acknowledgments	i
1	Grading Scales For Coins	1
2	US ½ Cent Liberty Cap	Pg 3
3	US ½ Cent Draped Bust	Pg 5
4	US ½ Cent Classic Head	Pg 7
5	US ½ Cent Braided Hair	Pg 9
6	US Large Cent Liberty Cap	Pg 11
7	US Large Cent Draped Bust	Pg 13
8	US Large Cent Classic Head	Pg 15
9	US Large Cent Liberty Matron Head	Pg 17
10	US Small Cent Flying Eagle	Pg 19
11	US Small Cent Indian Head	Pg 21
12	US Small Cent Lincoln Head Wheat Back	Pg 23
13	US Small Cent Lincoln Head Memorial Back	Pg 25
14	US Small Cent Lincoln Head Bicentennial Back	Pg 27
15	US Small Cent Lincoln Head Shield Back	Pg 29
16	US Two Cent	Pg 31
17	US Three Cent Silver (Trimes)	Pg 33
18	US Three Cent Nickel	Pg 35
19	US Five Cent Nickel Shield	Pg 37

20   US Five Cent Nickel Liberty Head   Pg 39

21   US Five Cent Nickel Indian Head   Pg 41

22   US Five Cent Nickel Jefferson Head   Pg 43

23   US Half Dimes Flowing   Pg 45
     Hair
     Draped Bust
24   US Half Dimes Capped   Pg 47
     Bust

25   US Half Dimes Liberty   Pg 49
     Seated

26   US Dimes Draped Bust   Pg 51

27   US Dimes Capped Bust   Pg 53

28   US Dimes Liberty Seated   Pg 55

29   US Dimes Barber Head   Pg 57

30   US Dimes Winged Liberty   Pg 59
     Head

     Mercury

31   US Dimes Roosevelt   Pg 61

32   US Twenty Cent Pieces   Pg 63

33   US Quarters Draped Bust   Pg 65

34   US Quarters Capped Bust   Pg 67

35   US Quarters Liberty   Pg 69
     Seated

36   US Quarters Barber   Pg 71

37   US Quarters Standing   Pg 73
     Liberty

38   Us Quarters Washington   Pg 75

39   US Quarters Washington   Pg 77

States

40	US Quarters Washington Territories America The Beautiful	Pg 79
41	US Half Dollars Flowing Hair	Pg 81
42	US Half Dollars Draped Bust	Pg 83
43	US Half Dollars Capped Bust	Pg 85
44	Us Half Dollars Liberty Seated	Pg 87
45	US Half Dollars Barber	Pg 89
46	US Half Dollars Walking Liberty	Pg 91
47	US Half Dollars Franklin	Pg 93
48	US Half Dollars Kennedy	Pg 95
49	US Dollars Flowing Hair	Pg 97

50   US Dollars Draped Bust   Pg 99

51   US Dollar Gobrecht   Pg 101

52   US Dollars Liberty Seated   Pg 103

53   US Dollars Trade Dollars   Pg 105

54   US Dollars Morgan   Pg 107

55   US Dollars Peace Dollars   Pg 109

56   US Dollars Eisenhower Eagle and Moon Reverse   Pg 111

57   US Dollars Susan B. Anthony   Pg 113

58   US Dollars Sacagawea   Pg 115

59   US Dollars Presidential   Pg 117

U S Coins Wanted

U S Coins Wanted

U S Coins Wanted

1. GRADING SCALES FOR COINS

What is a 70? NGC defines a Mint State or Proof 70 coin as having no post-production imperfections at 5x magnification.

vary to some degree because of blemishes, toning or slight imperfections as described in the following subdivisions:

Perfect Uncirculated (MS-70). Perfect new condition, showing no trace of wear. The finest quality possible, with no evidence of scratches, handling or contact with other coins. Very few regular issue coins are ever found in this condition.

Choice Uncirculated (MS-65). An above average Uncirculated coin which may be brilliant or lightly toned and has very few contact marks on the surface or rim. MS-67 through MS-62 indicate slightly higher or lower grades of preservation.

Uncirculated (MS-60). Has no trace of wear but may show a number of contact marks, and surface may be spotted or lack some luster.

Choice About Uncirculated (AU-55). Barest evidence of light wear on only the highest points of the design. Most of the mint luster remains.

About Uncirculated (AU-50). Has traces of light wear on many of the high points. At least half of the Mint luster is still present.

Choice Extremely Fine (EF-45). Light overall wear shows on highest points. All design details are very sharp. Some of the Mint luster is evident.

Extremely Fine (EF-40). Design is lightly worn throughout, but all features are sharp and well defined. Traces of luster may show.

Choice Very Fine (VF-30). Light even wear on the surface and highest parts of the design. All lettering and major features are sharp.

Very Fine (VF-20). A moderate amount of wear is noticeable on the high points of the coin's design. All major details are clear.

Fine (F-12). The coin shows moderate to considerable even wear throughout. Entire design is bold with an overall pleasing appearance.

Very Good (VG-8). Well worn with main features clear and bold although rather flat.

Good (G-4). Heavily worn with the design visible but faint in areas. Many details are flat. Common coins in "Good" condition are not particularly desirable pieces for collectors. Rare or valuable coins in this condition, however, are often saved when no others are available.

About Good (AG-3). Very heavily worn with portions of lettering date and legends worn smooth. The date may be barely readable.

2. U S ½ Cent

Liberty Cap- Facing Right 1794-97

DATE	CONDITION	NOTES

		4

3. U S ½ CENT

Draped Bust 1800-08

DATE	CONDITION	NOTES

		6

4. U S ½ Cent

Classic Head   1809-36

DATE	CONDITION	NOTES

		8

5. U S ½ CENT

Braided Hair   1840-57

DATE	CONDITION	NOTES

		10

6. U S Large Cent

Liberty Cap   1793-96

DATE	CONDITION	NOTES

		12

7. U S Large Cent

Draped Bust   1796-1807

DATE	CONDITION	NOTES

		14

8. U S Large Cent

Classic Head   1808-1814

DATE	CONDITION	NOTES

		16
		.

9. U S Large Cent

Liberty Head   1816-1857

(Matron Type 1816-35)

DATE	CONDITION	NOTES

		18

10. U S Small Cent

Flying Eagle   1856-1858

DATE	CONDITION	NOTES

		20

11. U S Small Cent

Indian Cents   1859-1909

DATE	CONDITION	NOTES

		22

12. U S Small Cent

Lincoln Head   1909-1958

Wheat Back

DATE	CONDITION	NOTES

13. U S Small Cent

Lincoln Head   1950-2008

Memorial Back

DATE	CONDITION	NOTES

		26

14. U S Small Cent

Lincoln Head   2009

Bicentennial Back

DATE	CONDITION	NOTES

		28

15. U S Small Cent

Lincoln Head   2010 -

Shield Back

DATE	CONDITION	NOTES

		30

16. U S Two Cent Piece

Two Cent 1864-1873

DATE	CONDITION	NOTES

		32

17. U S Three Cent Silver (Trimes)

Three Cent Silver 1851-1873

3 Varieties

DATE	CONDITION	NOTES

		34

18. U S Three Cent Nickel

Three Cent Nickel 1865-1889

DATE	CONDITION	NOTES

19. U S 5 Cent Nickel

Five Cent Nickel Shield 1866-1883

DATE	CONDITION	NOTES

		38

20. U S 5 Cent Nickel

Liberty Head 1883-1913

DATE	CONDITION	NOTES

		40

21. U S 5 Cent Nickel

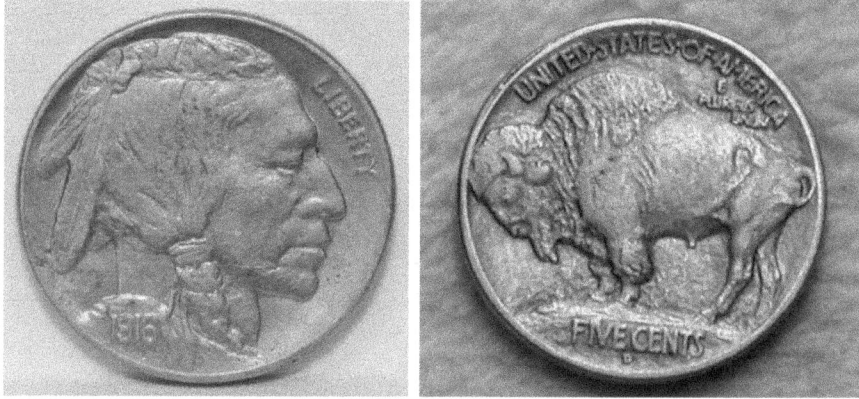

Indian Head 1913-1938

DATE	CONDITION	NOTES

		42

22. U S 5 Cent Nickel

Jefferson Head 1938 -

(Monticello and Westward Journey reverses)

DATE	CONDITION	NOTES

		44

23. U S Half Dimes

Flowing Hair 1794-95

Draped Bust 1796-1805

DATE	CONDITION	NOTES

		46

24. U S Half Dimes

Capped Bust 1829-1837

DATE	CONDITION	NOTES

		48

25. U S Half Dimes

Liberty Seated 1837-1873

DATE	CONDITION	NOTES

		50

26. U S Dimes

Draped Bust 1796-1807

DATE	CONDITION	NOTES

		52

27. U S Dimes

Capped Bust 1809-1837

DATE	CONDITION	NOTES

		54

28. U S Dimes

Liberty Seated 1837-1891

DATE	CONDITION	NOTES

		56

29. U S Dimes

Barber Head 1892-1916

DATE	CONDITION	NOTES

		58

30. U S Dimes

Winger Liberty Head 1916-1945

(Mercury Head)

DATE	CONDITION	NOTES

		60

31. U S Dimes

Roosevelt 1946-

DATE	CONDITION	NOTES

		62

32. U S Twenty –Cent Pieces

Liberty Seated 1875-1878

DATE	CONDITION	NOTES

		64

33. U S Quarters

Draped Bust 1796-1807

DATE	CONDITION	NOTES

		66

34. U S Quarters

Capped Bust 1815-1838

DATE	CONDITION	NOTES

		68

35. U S Quarters

Liberty Seated 1838-1891

DATE	CONDITION	NOTES

		70

36. U S Quarters

Barber 1892-1916

DATE	CONDITION	NOTES

		72

37. U S Quarters

Standing Liberty 1916-1930

DATE	CONDITION	NOTES

		74

38. U S Quarters

Washington 1932-

DATE	CONDITION	NOTES

39. U S Quarters

Washington State Quarters

1999-2008

DATE	CONDITION	NOTES

		78

40. U S Quarters

Washington Territories

America The Beautiful

2009 -2021

DATE	CONDITION	NOTES

		80

41. U S Half Dollar

Flowing Hair 1794-95

DATE	CONDITION	NOTES

		82

42. U S Half Dollar

Draped Bust 1796- 1807

DATE	CONDITION	NOTES

		84

43. U S Half Dollar

Capped Bust 1807- 1836

Lettered Edge

Reeded Edge 1836-39

DATE	CONDITION	NOTES

		86

44. U S Half Dollar

Liberty Seated 1839-1891

DATE	CONDITION	NOTES

		88

45. U S Half Dollar

Barber 1892-1915

DATE	CONDITION	NOTES

		90

46. U S Half Dollar

Walking Liberty 1816-1947

DATE	CONDITION	NOTES

		92

47. U S Half Dollar

Franklin 1948-1963

DATE	CONDITION	NOTES

		94

48. U S Half Dollar

Kennedy 1964 -

DATE	CONDITION	NOTES

		96

49. U S Dollar

Flowing Hair 1794-95

DATE	CONDITION	NOTES

		98

50. U S Dollar

Draped Bust 1795- 1804

DATE	CONDITION	NOTES

51. U S Dollar

Gobrecht Dollars 1836-39

DATE	CONDITION	NOTES

		102

52. U S Dollar

Liberty Seated 1840-73

DATE	CONDITION	NOTES

		104

53. U S Dollar

Trade Dollars 1873-85

DATE	CONDITION	NOTES

		106

54. U S Dollar

Morgan 1878-1921

DATE	CONDITION	NOTES

55. U S Dollar

Peace Dollar 1921-1935

DATE	CONDITION	NOTES

56. U S Dollar

Eisenhower 1971-1978

(Eagle reverse 1971-74)

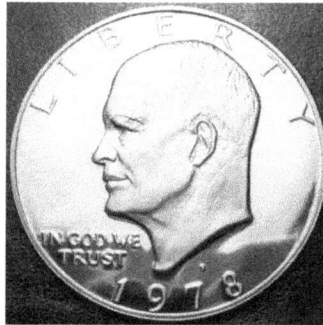

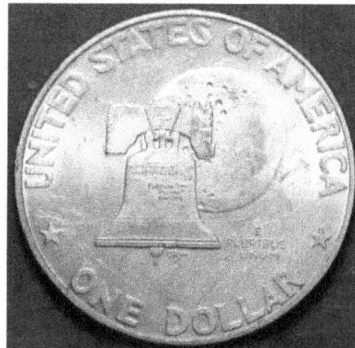

DATE	CONDITION	NOTES

57. U S Dollar

Susan B. Anthony 1979-1999

DATE	CONDITION	NOTES

		114

58. U S Dollar

Sacagawea 2000-

2009   2010   2011   2012   2013

DATE	CONDITION	NOTES

		116

59. U S Dollar

Presidential 2007-20016

DATE	CONDITION	NOTES

		118

ABOUT THE AUTHOR

Thomas Saunders-BIO

Thomas Saunders of Whitmore Lake is a long time writer and publisher of humor and niche books. In 2005 Tom was one of the winners of the Robert Benchley Award for Humor. He became a member of the Robert Benchley Society board of Directors in 2006 and is the president of the local chapter of the Benchley Society, "A Moderate State Of Preservation" in Ann Arbor. The quote is from Benchley's article, "No Pullmans, Please!" In addition he is the editor of the Benchley Journal, an annual publication dedicated to the Robert Benchley Writing contest. He published 'The Athletic Benchley-105 Exercises from The Detroit Athletic Club News" in 2010 for which he won two national awards; The Midwest Book Awards-Humor and the National Indie Excellence Award for Humor in 2011.

Tom has collected coins starting at age 8 with the gift of three Indian Head pennies from his grand mother. He since has gone on to collect US coins and English and Canadian coins. He is a member of the American Numismatic Association (R-1165061) and the Michigan State Numismatic Society (10220). Currently he is working on completing the Shield Nickel series.

www.ingramcontent.com/pod-product-compliance
Lightning Source LLC
Chambersburg PA
CBHW080935040426
42443CB00015B/3424